What Happened at Roswell?

BY GEORGE DUDDING

PUBLISHED BY GSD PUBLICATIONS
Spencer, West Virginia
May 7, 2013

http://www.gdparanormal.com

In Memory of Pamela Jane Dudding
1957-2012

Graphics Design and Publishing Assistance
by John Dudding

No. 2013-004

TABLE OF CONTENTS

STORMS OVER NEW MEXICO 1

DISCOVERY ON THE FOSTER RANCH 3

INVOLVEMENT BY THE RAAF.......................6

A CHANGE OF STORIES...14

KNOWLEDGE OF MILITARY PERSONNEL 17

WITNESS TESTIMONY..20

POLITICS AND UFOs...32

COVER-UPS AND PROJECT MOGUL 35

BOOKS, TELEVISION, AND POP CULTURE 37

CONCLUSION...40

MAP OF WHERE IT HAPPENED
FROM U.S. AIR FORCE DOCUMENT

What Happened At Roswell?

"I heard you had reports this morning of an unidentified aircraft. Don't worry it was just me."

-George W. Bush in speech at Roswell, New Mexico (2004)

STORMS OVER NEW MEXICO

Thunder echoed overhead, and rain began to pour downward onto the hot, dry ground as a storm moved in to cool off and replace the heat that had stifled this southwestern United States community for over a month now. It was the night of July 2, 1947, and Mr. and Mrs. Dan Wilmot stood outside on their porch looking up into the sky. Suddenly, something large, glowing, and in the shape of a disk appeared above them. It was moving swiftly through the atmosphere as it passed over their house, heading along a northwestward trajectory above Roswell,

New Mexico. The strange craft was tracing a path in the direction of Corona, New Mexico, 100 miles away. Shortly, the disk-shaped object exploded in the air, far away above the sparsely inhabited and arid ranchland typical of the geographical region. Little did the observers know that the events which were unfolding before their very eyes would mystify countless curious individuals for many years to come—forever leaving scores of unanswered questions.

Very shortly, another person, about 60 miles away up toward Corona, New Mexico, also thought he heard an explosion overhead above the line shack where he was living. He went back inside and decided that it was all part of the raging thunderstorm. He was mainly concerned with the welfare of a huge herd of sheep that fell under his responsibility. The man was 48-year-old William Ware "Mack" Brazel, a foreman on the mammoth J.B. Foster Ranch up near Corona. Brazel was living on the ranch in a tiny isolated shack with no conveniences such as electricity, phone, or running water. If something major was to happen, he was cut off from the rest of the world until he could make it to a nearby town. His nearest neighbors were Floyd and Loretta Proctor, about ten miles away. His wife and family were living in better conditions back in

Tularosa, New Mexico because he wanted the children to be able to attend better schools. On that night, it is believed that two of his children, along with the neighboring Proctor boy, were staying with him at the remote ranch outpost.

DISCOVERY ON THE FOSTER RANCH

It was bright and early the next morning on July 3, 1947 when Brazel decided to check on his herd of sheep. Accompanied by seven-year-old Tommy D. Proctor, son of neighbors Floyd and Loretta Proctor, he mounted his horse and headed out onto the range to locate the herd of sheep. They needed to be rounded up and moved to a different pasture. The two herders had been riding their horses for quite some time, when they came upon a large amount of debris scattered across the pasture field. There appeared to be a gouged-out trench, which reached for a lengthy distance across the field and then down one hillside, across to another. It seemed that some type of craft had crashed into the ground and skidded for several hundred feet. Fragments, of metal, large and small, were scattered around, along with other forms of strange material. Brazel picked up various pieces of the wreckage and noticed that the metal was extremely light yet strong. It behaved strangely, when twisted and bent, by returning to its original shape. Some of the metal was in the form of sheets, while some was in the form of thin I-beams with strange hieroglyphic characters visibly printed on their exterior. He gathered up a bundle of larger pieces, returned with them to his residence, and placed part of the debris in an old barn located nearby.

Brazel took several pieces of the metal and drove over to the Proctors to see what they had to say. Floyd and Loretta Proctor told him that there had been a large number of flying disk, or UFO, sightings recently in the news, beginning with one spotted by a private pilot up around Mt. Ranier, Washington. They explained that this could be part of a flying saucer, or some type of secret experimental craft that the government was working on. They recommended that he report it to the authorities as soon as possible because someone needed to know about it.

It was around July 5, 1947 when Brazel drove up to the nearby town of Corona and saw a reward poster in the amount of $3,000 for anyone finding a flying saucer or disk. He was beginning to think that he had definitely found one, plus he also needed money for a new truck. Corona was such a small place, so Brazel knew he was going to have to go to Roswell and speak to the proper authorities. On July 6, 1947, he drove down to Roswell and met with Sheriff George Wilcox to explain what he had found on the ranch. He intended to leave some of the wreckage debris at the Sheriff's office to be examined. After Sheriff Wilcox looked at the strange pieces of metallic debris, he decided that there was something of importance there. Suddenly, the phone rang, and the sheriff answered it. On the phone was Frank Joyce, who happened to be a radio reporter and disk jockey from *KGFL* radio, which was located there in Roswell. Joyce had called to ask if there was anything newsworthy that day. The sheriff told him that Mack Brazel was in his office with a bizarre story. He handed the phone over to Brazel, who then related the entire story and described what he had found on the Foster ranch near Corona.

Shortly, Sheriff Wilcox accompanied himself with some deputies and went out to the Foster ranch to look at the crash site. Once there, they found exactly what Brazel had described to them. There was a blackened site with metal debris scattered all over the pasture land. Wilcox thought things over and decided that he needed help from some kind of higher up authorities or experts. The 509th Bomber Group, which was known for its nuclear capability and the origin of the flight that dropped two atomic bombs on Japan, was based at the Roswell Army Air Field (later named Walker Air Force Base). Sheriff Wilcox contacted Colonel William Blanchard, Commander at the Roswell Army Air Field (RAAF), and updated him on what was going on. Colonel Blanchard then instructed Major Jesse Marcel and Captain Sheridan Cavitt of the Counter Intelligence Corps (CIC) to check out the story. Marcel and Cavitt went to the Sheriff's office and picked up the crash debris left there by Brazel. Upon examination of the pieces, they knew that they were on to something. They felt the urgency to get out to the alleged crash site as they wanted to do an investigation to see just exactly what they had on their hands.

INVOLVEMENT BY THE RAAF

It was on July 7, 1947 when Marcel and Cavitt drove two vehicles, a car and a jeep, out to the Foster ranch to pick up the debris which Brazel had in a building next to his house. They stayed all night at the ranch because it was too late in the evening to go out onto the range where the crash site was located. The next morning, on July 8, 1947, they went out to the crash site, gathered up as much of the material as they could, and loaded it into their vehicles to be taken back to Roswell Army Air Field. As Marcel later told, it was his opinion that the strange material found at the Foster ranch did not originate from here on Earth. Did the military believe that they had found the wreckage of a flying saucer?

Another finding at the site revealed that the wreckage did not extend only a few hundred feet but was strung out in a path about 300 feet wide and 0.75 miles long. On Marcel's return trip to the RAAF with his vehicle loaded with wreckage, he did a strange thing that would be of significance later on. He sent Cavitt on to the base while he stopped off at his house and showed the strange material to his wife and son, Jesse Marcel, Jr. His son told the story in later years and was able to add to the presently ongoing and never ending investigation.

At the RAAF base, Colonel William Blanchard instructed Lieutenant Walter Haut to prepare a press release stating that a flying saucer (crashed disk) had landed or crashed in the desert and that the government had it in their possession. The press release was sent out on the news wire service, and within hours, according to sources, it is believed that over thirty newspapers published headlines that a saucer had landed. Headlines in the July 8, 1947 edition of the *Roswell Daily Record* read, *"RAAF Captures Flying Saucer on Ranch in Roswell Region."* Another story on the front page stated, *"No Details of Flying Disk Are Revealed,"* and *"Roswell Hardware Man and Wife Report Disk Seen."* Radio stations also carried the saucer news.

NEWSPAPER FRONT PAGE DETAILING EVENT
ROSWELL DAILY RECORD - JULY 8, 1947

Immediately, the Roswell Army Air Field dispatched military troops, trucks, ambulances, jeeps, and personnel carriers onto the Foster ranch to begin a rescue and recovery operation. Major Edwin Easley was placed in charge of both securing the site and keeping unauthorized spectators from seeing what was happening. He ordered barricades, manned by military police, to be erected on all roads coming in and out of the Foster ranch. The entire area was restricted to military personnel only, and all civilians were excluded in order to keep any type of information or material from leaving the alleged crash site. Special investigators and photographers from Washington, D.C., along with representatives of President Truman, arrived shortly. Military troops were dispatched, and all roads into the area were blocked off by military police. President Truman sent his representatives to the scene as this was considered a matter of national security. Soldiers swarmed the area, gathering up every bit of the crash material they could find. Surveillance planes flew overhead looking for anything unusual that might have been missed. Then, unexpectedly, they spotted something located several miles away. It seemed that there was some type of shiny reflection which led them to a downed craft. According to various sources, it is said that a flying saucer was lodged in a huge embankment and that there were also bodies at that site. Some stories say that there were several dead alien beings and one that was still alive. One individual, Sgt. Melvin Brown, a member of the military police, later claimed he saw alien bodies concealed under a tarpaulin on the back of an army truck. All of the crash debris, flying saucer remains, and alleged bodies were transported by military trucks and ambulances to Hangar 84 at the RAAF in Roswell for safekeeping. Military police, including Sgt. Brown who was mentioned above, were placed around the hangar to keep people out.

CURTIS E. LEMAY AND ROGER M. RAMEY
U.S. AIR FORCE PHOTO

COLONEL WILLIAM H. BLANCHARD
U.S. AIR FORCE PHOTO

Later that same day, Colonel Blanchard received special orders from General Roger M. Ramey, Commander of the 8th Air Force at Fort Worth Army Air Field (later named Carswell Air Force Base) in Fort Worth, Texas. The orders stated that he was to bring some of the crash

11

debris there immediately. General Ramey also put out a press release stating that an error had been made in an earlier report and that a weather balloon had been found at the Foster ranch, not a flying saucer. The headlines in the next issue of the *Roswell Daily Record* on July 9, 1947 read, *"Gen. Ramey Empties Roswell Saucer,"* and another smaller sub-headline said, *"Ramey Says Excitement Is Not Justified."* Another Roswell newspaper, the *Roswell Morning Dispatch* read, *"Army Debunks Roswell Flying Disk As World Simmers With Excitement,"* while a smaller sub-headline read, *"Officers Say Disk Is Weather Balloon."*

NEWSPAPER STORY DENYING SAUCER CAPTURE
ROSWELL DAILY RECORD - JULY 9, 1947

Some of the recovered flying saucer remains was placed on a B-29 bomber and was then flown to Fort Worth Army Air Field, along with Major Jesse Marcel. Upon arrival at Fort Worth, a sample of the crash debris was taken to General Roger Ramey's office by Major Marcel. General Ramey examined the material and then requested that Major Marcel accompany him to a room down the hall in order to show him on a map exactly where the crash had occurred. According to later testimony by Major Marcel, when he returned with General Ramey to his office, the flying saucer debris which he had brought with him had been replaced by what appeared to be a weather balloon with a radar target attached! Major Marcel claimed that he objected and stated to Ramey that it was not the same material that he had brought to the office. According to further testimony later given by Marcel, General Ramey told him that it was the exact same material and was definitely confirmed to be a weather balloon with a radar target attached. Furthermore, Marcel was instructed to hold up part of the weather balloon and join him in a photo session. Ramey and Marcel then posed together with Marcel holding pieces of the weather balloon, and their photographs were taken by a photographer later identified as James Bond Johnson of the *Fort Worth Star-Telegram*.

I would like to mention in this book that Ramey is seen holding a piece of paper in one of the photographs. It is claimed, in some UFO research documents, that forensic experts have enlarged the note. Then, by rotating it and using special techniques, they have enhanced the message to a point that it can be read. It is thereby claimed that the message is some kind of memo stating that a flying disk has crashed and that alien bodies have been recovered.

To continue, Marcel later stated that a cover-up took place and that he was forced to go along with the weather balloon story. One problem with the object being a weather balloon is that the balloon was reported as being 20 to 25 feet in diameter with a radar reflector attached, and yet, the crash debris was scattered over such a large area of almost a square mile. There simply was not enough material in a weather balloon to leave behind the amount of material recovered.

A CHANGE OF STORIES

It was on the same day of July 8, 1947 when Frank Joyce, the *KGFL* radio reporter who had initially interviewed Mac Brazel about the saucer crash, informed his boss, Walt Whitmore, about Brazel's story. Whitmore drove out to the Foster ranch to meet with Brazel in order to obtain a more thorough interview. At that time, Brazel accompanied Whitmore back to Roswell, where a recorded interview was conducted. An old-fashioned, wire-type recorder that used magnetic wire instead of magnetic tape was used to record the interview. For some reason, Whitmore was never able to release that interview. Whitmore claimed that he was going to air the entire recorded interview but was told not to do so by undisclosed authorities. He also claimed that the Federal Communications Commission told him that they would pull his radio station license if the interview aired.

Sometime shortly after that interview, it is said that military police took Brazel into custody and held him at the RAAF military base. Brazel later claimed that they told him not to talk about the crash, or anything which had occurred on his ranch. They also accompanied him to radio station *KGFL*, where he had previously released his story about the flying saucer crash. They supposedly told him to tell them a different story about what he had found. The new story was that it was a weather balloon, and not a flying saucer, that was found out at the J.B. Foster ranch. Upon completing the requested task and leaving the radio station, he was once again accompanied by military police and escorted to the military base, where he was held for about three more days.

After Brazel was released, people tried to ask him questions about what had happened, but he would not talk about it. He stated that he had been told not to discuss the incident anymore. The July 9, 1947 edition of the *Roswell Daily Record* headlines read, *"Harassed Rancher Who Located 'Saucer' Sorry He Told About It."* There seemed to be a full blown cover-up being put in place.

Harassed Rancher who Located 'Saucer' Sorry He Told About It

W. W. Brazel, 48, Lincoln county rancher living 30 miles south east of Corona, today told his story of finding what the army at first described as a flying disk, but the publicity which attended his find caused him to add that if he ever found anything else short of a bomb he sure wasn't going to say anything about it.

Brazel was brought here late yesterday by W. E. Whitmore, of radio station KGFL, had his picture taken and gave an interview to the Record and Jason Kellahin, sent here from the Albuquerque bureau of the Associated Press to cover the story. The picture he posed for was sent out over AP telephoto wire tending machine specially set up in the Record office by R. D. Adair, AP wire chief sent here from Albuquerque for the sole purpose of getting out his picture and that of sheriff George Wilcox, to whom Brazel originally gave the information of his find.

Brazel related that on June 14 he and an 8-year old son, Vernon were about 7 or 8 miles from the ranch house of the J. B. Foster ranch, which he operates, when they came upon a large area of bright wreckage made up on rubber strips, tinfoil, a rather tough paper and sticks.

At the time Brazel was in a hurry to get his round-mado and he did not pay much attention to it. But he did remark about when he/had seen and on July 4 he, his wife, Vernon and a daughter Betty, age 14, went back to the spot and gathered up quite a bit of the debris.

The next day he first heard about the flying disks, and he wondered if what he had found might be the remnants of one of these.

Monday he came to town to sell some wool and when here he went to see sheriff George Wilcox and "whispered kinda confidential like" that he might have found a flying disk.

Wilcox got in touch with the Roswell Army Air Field and Maj. Jesse A. Marcel and a man in plain clothes accompanied him home, where they picked up the rest of the pieces of the "disk" and went to his home to try to reconstruct it.

According to Brazel they simply could not reconstruct it at all. They tried to make a kite out of it, but could not do that and could not find any way to put it back together so that it would fit.

Then Major Marcel brought it to Roswell and that was the last he heard of it until the story broke that he had found a flying disk.

Brazel said that he did not see it fall from the sky and did not see it before it was torn up, so he did not know the size or shape it might have been, but he thought it might have been about as large as a table top. The balloon which held it up, if that was how it worked, must have been about 12 feet long, he felt, measuring the distance by the size of the room in which he sat. The rubber was smoky gray in color and scattered over an area about 200 yards in diameter.

When the debris was gathered up the tinfoil, paper, tape, and sticks made a bundle about three feet long and 7 or 8 inches thick, while the rubber made a bundle about 18 or 20 inches long and about 8 inches thick. In all, he estimated, the entire lot would have weighed maybe five pounds.

There was no sign of any metal in the area which might have been used for an engine and no sign of any propellers of any kind, although at least one paper fin had been glued onto some of the tinfoil.

There were no words to be found anywhere on the instrument, although there were letters on some of the parts. Considerable scotch tape and some tape with flowers printed upon it had been used in the construction.

No strings or wire were to be found but there were some eyelets in the paper to indicate that some sort of attachment may have been used.

Brazel said that he had previously found two weather observation balloons on the ranch, but that what he found this time did not in any way resemble either of these.

"I am sure what I found was not any weather observation balloon," he said. "But if I find anything else, besides a bomb they are going to have a hard time getting me to say anything about it."

MAC BRAZEL ARTICLE
ROSWELL DAILY RECORD - JULY 9, 1947

In later years, Brazel said that he had seen enough weather balloons land on the ranch, and this was not one of them. Several years later, Mack's son Bill Brazel revealed that he was still in possession of a few pieces of the debris which he had found years before. He stated that a couple of military officers came to the house and requested that he hand over the fragments and that he cooperated because he was afraid of getting into trouble for having them in his possession.

There are other stories which have been told about military personnel raiding newspaper offices and radio stations, going through desks and file cabinets, and telling members of the news media that they were not to discuss or divulge any more information. Some have even claimed that they received death threats discouraging them from revealing any information on the flying saucer crash incident!

KNOWLEDGE OF MILITARY PERSONNEL

For the next few days, military officials continued to scour the crash site to gather up all pieces of the object. They then boxed them up and moved them to Hangar 84 at RAAF in Roswell. Every last piece of material, along with reported remains of alien bodies, was placed onboard Boeing B-29 and Douglas C-54 planes and flown to Wright Field (later named Wright-Patterson Air Force Base) in Dayton, Ohio. In later years, Captain Oliver W. Henderson is reported to have told that he flew a C-54 from Roswell to Wright Field and that the cargo was flying saucer debris and alien bodies packed in dry ice.

Something suspicious had definitely taken place. First, the Army had put out a press release that a flying saucer had been recovered but, within hours, had changed the story to a weather balloon being found. Would there be more changes to their story in the future? I think you, the reader, can guess the answer to that question. Later testimonials given by military officials would further indicate a cover-up in the Roswell incident.

General Thomas DuBose stated that, in 1947, he was a Colonel, serving as General Ramey's Chief of Staff at Fort Worth, Texas. In later years, DuBose stated that he received a phone call directly from General Clements McMullen at Andrews Army Air Field (later name Andrews Air Force Base) located in Washington, D.C. Orders were given to General Ramey that he was to come up with a story to throw off newspaper reporters and civilians. In other words, he was directed straight from the top to invent some type of cover-up story.

First Lieutenant Robert Shirkey, an operations officer for the 509th Bomb Group at the RAAF, later stated that he saw boxes of debris being loaded on a B-29 bomber to be hauled to Fort Worth. Due to his intense interest in what was taking place and the fact that he had seen too much, he claimed that he was quickly transferred, by order of General Ramey, to an insignificant position at a remote location in the Philippines. He had been expecting to be promoted to the rank of Captain but ended up being an officer of weights and measures.

Lieutenant Arthur E. Exon was located at Wright Field in Dayton, Ohio in July of 1947, when the material was transported to that base. He later said that a number of tests were conducted on the "saucer" material. It did not react chemically to other substances, behaved strangely, and had enormous tensile strength. One of the panels was reportedly subjected to the impact of a sledge hammer and would not dent. Exon stated that the people who tested it pretty much agreed that it was something from another world.

WITNESS TESTIMONY

Another radio station cover-up story involved a woman named Lydia Sleppy, who was working at the *KOAT* radio station in Albuquerque, New Mexico on or around July 8, 1947. She stated that she had received a phone call from John McBoyle, part owner of the *RSWX* radio station in Roswell, informing her of a story he had just heard about a flying saucer and the recovery of alien bodies near Roswell. She stated that she took down the story and was trying to put it on the teletype to ABC News when the FBI came on the line, interrupted her transmission, and told her to stop transmitting any such information. Concerning this story, there has been additional questions about how the teletype transmission could have been interrupted without switching the device into receive mode. Also, archives of FBI records do not show that any such message was sent— but do you really expect them to release those records, if they even exist?

Paul Wilmot, the son of Mr. and Mrs. Dan Wilmot, was interviewed by Jesse Marcel, Jr. years later. He told about the night his parents saw the flying disk pass over Roswell on its northwest trajectory toward Corona and how it then exploded in the sky.

Glenn Dennis, a local mortician who worked at the Ballard Funeral Home in Roswell during 1947, came forward in later years claiming that he was contacted by the RAAF during that time and asked if he had several small coffins available. He claimed that he informed them that he could obtain whatever they needed. They also inquired regarding how bodies which had already started decomposing could be preserved for shipping. He said that he recommended that they pack the bodies in dry ice. At that time, Dennis stated that he was curious about what was going on because the RAAF generally used the mortuary services of Ballard Funeral Home whenever it was needed. He then drove over to the base hospital to see what was going on. Upon arrival, he saw several ambulances pulled up out front of the hospital with the back doors open. He peered inside them and saw a lot of metal debris. Deciding to go inside to see what was going on, he observed a nurse coming out of a room. He recognized the nurse, but she told him that he needed to leave immediately as he was going to get into trouble for being there. She told him that she would meet him in town to explain more clearly. Suddenly, several military police officers grabbed him, asked him what he was doing there, and ordered him to leave. They then grabbed him by the arms, with one on each side, and forcibly escorted him outside the building. Later, back in town, he met up with the nurse at a cafe, and she told him that she had been told not to reveal anything about what was going on. She explained to him that she had assisted in the performance of autopsies on alien bodies which had been recovered from a flying saucer crash. Dennis claimed that he never saw the nurse again and that she was supposedly transferred to another base somewhere in England. Dennis claimed that he tried to contact her, but his letter was returned. He later stated that he was told that she was killed in a plane crash. At first, Dennis refused to tell her name but later identified her as Naomi Maria Selff. No records can be found on that name. At some point since then, Dennis has stated that he gave a fictitious name because he had promised not to reveal her identity. Today, UFO investigators think they may have determined that her real name was Mary Lowe, a nurse who worked on the base at that time. There have been several theories as to the correct nurse identity. Glenn Dennis later joined up with Walter Haut, a key witness mentioned earlier in this book, and became one of the founders of the International UFO Museum and Research Center in Roswell.

Earlier in this book, I mentioned the Brazel debris field and the discovery of a crash site several miles away. Those sites would be about 60 miles northwest of Roswell, New Mexico, close to Corona, New Mexico. To complicate matters, it is now believed that there was a second crash site with its location being another mystery. Fifty years after the crash, Frank J. Kaufmann came forward and told a story about how a crash had shown up on a radar screen. He stated that he was dispatched, along with a crew of military personnel from the Roswell Army Air Field, to a site about 20 miles northwest of Roswell. It was there that they found a crashed flying saucer embedded into a high embankment, or arroyo as it is called. There were five alien bodies present at the site. Kaufmann told that the dead aliens were placed in body bags and transported back to the base. The flying saucer, which was in the shape of a half crescent according to his description, was loaded on a large flatbed truck and covered with a tarpaulin. The craft was then hauled back to the base. The bodies and craft were placed inside Hangar 84 at the RAAF base. Kaufmann claimed that he secretly kept this information for years. When witnesses began coming forth, he decided that since he was getting old, it was time to let the public know what really truly happened. The site described above is located on a 15,000-acre ranch, presently owned by Miller "Hub" Corn and formerly owned by the McKnight family at the time of the incident. It is currently a tourist site frequented by UFO enthusiasts and visitors to Roswell and is open by admission.

Another witness has surfaced to confirm the Frank Kaufmann site. James Ragsdale came forward in 1993 and stated that on the night of the Roswell crash, he was camping in the desert with a girl named Trudy Truelove (believed to be a fake name). Sometime before midnight, a flaming object passed overhead and crashed about a mile from their campsite. Ragsdale and Truelove got in his truck and went to investigate. Upon their arrival, they saw that some type of object had crashed into the side of a cliff and was lodged there. It was too dark to explore, so they returned to camp and waited until the following morning. For some reason, they did not return immediately back to town and summon help. The next morning, they went back to the crash site and found a strange flying saucer type craft with multiple strange-looking bodies scattered around outside. After collecting some debris, they saw a cloud of dust moving in their direction. Acting quickly, Ragsdale and Truelove moved their truck to a distant grove of trees. Ragsdale claimed that a convoy of army trucks and vehicles, along with military personnel, came to the scene, gathered up the bodies, and loaded the saucer onto a large flatbed truck. The military crew cleaned up every bit of the crash debris and then left. Ragsdale claimed that he and Truelove kept some of the debris from the site. He further claimed that Truelove wrecked her car and was killed several months later, and as far as he knew, the debris in her possession was lost after her car was towed away. Unsurprisingly, his truck was stolen, and the remaining debris was lost with the truck, which was never found. The crash site he described coincided with the one at the Miller "Hub" Corn ranch. Later in 1995, Ragsdale changed part of his story for some reason and placed the crash site about 50 or 60 miles west of Roswell. UFO investigators were confused about this change of story.

Another witness, William M. Woody, stated in 1993 that he was 12 years old at the time of the UFO landing in Roswell and lived on a farm near Roswell. He said that on the night of the crash, he and his father saw a bright fireball travel across the sky going northwest and that it seemed to land north of town. The next morning, he went with his father up Route 285, about 20 miles north of Roswell. They came upon military personnel posted all along the highway at side roads and ranch entrances all the way up to Route 247, which turns toward Corona. The military was guarding the whole area and making sure no one left the highway, venturing into the surrounding countryside. He said that his father turned around about ten miles north of Route 247 and returned to Roswell.

In 1978, Jean and Verne Maltais reported that a friend of theirs had confided in them several years after the Roswell incident that he had been working as an engineer for the United States Soil Conservation Service at an area near Magdalena, New Mexico on the Plains of San Agustin (sometimes spelled Augustin) in July of 1947. The government was providing services to farmers and ranchers to help them preserve soil and water as a result of what happened during the "Dust Bowl" of the 1930s. The engineer was Grady L. Barnett (Barney Barnett), who further stated that he saw something shiny in the desert during his travels from ranch to ranch and drove out to see what it was. What he found was a crashed flying saucer about 6 feet tall, 25 feet in diameter, and split open on the side. There were several dead non-human bodies lying both inside and outside the craft. He reported that several archaeology students who had been working at a nearby prehistoric dwelling possibly known as "Bat Cave" arrived a little later and also looked over the crash. A short time later, U.S. Army personnel arrived and took over the site to begin cleanup and removal. Individuals were called aside and told that it was a matter of national security and that they were never to tell about or discuss what they had seen. People at that time understood matters of national security and were more likely to cooperate than people of this day and age.

Another crash witness, who surfaced in 1990, confirmed the above story. Gerald Anderson stated that he was about six years old in July of 1947 and was with his brother, his father, an uncle, and a cousin out in the desert area of western New Mexico known as the Plains of San Agustin near Magdalena, New Mexico. They were engaged in a search for moss agate, a semi-precious gemstone. Anderson stated that they came upon a crashed flying saucer and that there were also several alien bodies lying around. He further stated that while they were there, several college students and a professor that were doing archaeological work at the nearby cliff dwellings came along. Then, after that, a soil conservation specialist named Barney Barnett arrived. Shortly, military vehicles and personnel showed up and took charge of the site. Military police made them all leave, just as they always do in all of these government cover-up conspiracies.

There are now four possible crash sites. The first site was a short distance from the Brazel debris field on the Foster ranch. The second site is on the Miller "Hub" Corn ranch. The third site is the final Ragsdale site, and the fourth site is on the Plains of San Agustin. The Foster ranch site and the Plains of San Agustin are considered by many to be the accepted crash sites.

In 1998, retired Army Colonel Philip J. Corso made a statement that the wreckage from the Roswell site was not a weather balloon and that it was an extraterrestrial spacecraft. He also claimed that he saw the body of a dead alien while stationed at Fort Riley in Kansas. He told that he was curious about several large boxes or crates which were stored in a top secret area. He pried one of the crates open and found a sealed glass container containing a strange body immersed in some type of preservative fluid. He described the body to be about four feet tall with an odd-shaped head that you would normally associate with a space alien. The body had skinny arms and hands with four fingers. He stated that he also saw top secret documents at the Pentagon, which referred to the Roswell flying saucer and its associated alien bodies. According to Corso, the alien bodies were brought to Walter Reed General Hospital in Washington, D.C. for examination. Furthermore, Corso claimed that the United States government and Department of Defense "reverse engineered" alien spacecraft technology to make such things as transistors, integrated circuits, lasers, fiber optics, strong fibers (such as those used in bullet-proof vests), and modern weapons. He claimed that the technology was given to various companies to manufacture and market related products. Corso had an impressive military history, having worked under General Douglas MacArthur and as President Dwight D. Eisenhower's national security staff. There seems to be no reason that he would make this kind of story up.

Another individual who came to light with a similar "reverse engineering" testimony was Robert Lazar. In the 1980s, Lazar came forward with claims that he had worked as a scientist and engineer at a site known as S4, located near Area 51 at Groom Lake in the Nevada desert. Lazar told that the S4 site was a highly-camouflaged location built inside a mountain. He said that he saw several extraterrestrial crafts at the site and that he personally worked on reverse engineering the alien technology from those crafts so that the government and military could put it to use. Lazar stated that he worked with an engine from the alien vehicles powered by using Element 115. At that time, there was no element with an atomic number of 115 on the periodic table of elements. Since then, around 1994, physicists at Lawrence Livermore National Laboratories in the United States and at the Joint Institute for Nuclear Research in Dubna, Russia have proved its existence by bombarding an Americium-224 atom with a Calcium-48 ion to produce four atoms of Element 115 (Ununpentium), which has a half-life of between 20 and 650 milliseconds, depending on its isotope. It has been determined that Area 51 exists, and in some documentation, there might be references to an S4 site. However, there have been multiple questions about the science background of Robert Lazar. Lazar, according to some accounts, claimed that he had degrees from MIT (Massachusetts Institute of Technology) and Caltech (California Institute of Technology), two of the top schools in the United States. It is claimed that no records of Lazar attending those two institutions can be found. Lazar also claims to have worked at other top secret government institutions. Anti-UFO researchers who are trying to disprove witness testimonies are constantly trying to dig up evidence to counteract them.

However, when researching Lazar, his name has turned up on employee directories at some of those places, which may seem to vouch for his claims. Conspiracy theorists believe that Lazar's records have been erased from schools and top secret government installations as part of the cover-up.

What happened to the crash debris and saucer which was sent to Wright Field in Dayton, Ohio? June Crain came forth in 1997 and stated that, due to her age, she was telling the story of when she worked at Wright-Patterson Air Force Base (Wright Field) from 1942 until 1952. Crain was a secretary at the base and stated that three flying saucer vehicles had been brought to the base during the time she worked there and that one was from Roswell. She also stated that some alien bodies had been brought there and placed in cold storage. She said that she knew about the alien bodies through co-workers and from documents which she had to type, process, and file. She stated that one of her superiors brought a piece of the crash debris to her office and that it displayed strange properties. Crain stated that everyone was required to sign documents agreeing to keep their knowledge of the extraterrestrial crafts, materials, and aliens confidential. June Crain died about a year after making her statement to UFO investigators.

In 2007, on the 60th anniversary of the Roswell crash, a new witness came forward with information about his involvement in the Roswell crash. Earl Fulford claimed that he was a Staff Sergeant at the RAAF in 1947. He stated that he had kept all of his knowledge a secret for years because all military personnel were sworn to secrecy at the time, and none of them were about to reveal anything they knew because of the possibility of reprisals. He appeared on Larry King Live and spoke at the International UFO Museum and Research Center at Roswell. He stated that he decided to reveal his experience because he did not think there was anything anyone could do to him at his age. He told of the appearance of UFOs in the sky around Roswell at the time and also about being sent out in the field with a crew of others to gather up the debris from the crash site while being supervised by higher-up officers and military police.

POLITICS AND UFOs

In the early 1990s, brothers Ruben and Pete Anaya claimed that, on July 7, 1947, they received a call from Lieutenant Governor Joseph Montoya of New Mexico. He requested that they come immediately and pick him up at RAAF Hangar 84. The two drove to Hangar 84 at the base, where they met Montoya and then drove him back to their house. Montoya, who was at the base for the dedication of a new plane, told them he had seen the flying saucer and the dead alien bodies housed in the hangar. Montoya is reported to have told them to keep this information quiet. They were also contacted by other government officials about keeping it a secret due to national security. Later, in the 1960s, Montoya became a U.S. Senator.

Another politician who became involved in the Roswell search for truth was Congressman Steve Schiff of New Mexico. In the early 1990s, he attempted to get the Pentagon to release all information about the Roswell incident but was unsuccessful due to claims of national security. Undeterred, he attempted to get the Government Accounting Office (GAO) to investigate the matter. In the end, the GAO said that most of the Roswell records had been lost or destroyed. In a political cartoon at that time, Hillary Clinton is telling Bill Clinton that Congressman Schiff is demanding a full disclosure of what happened at Roswell. Bill, thinking that he is being accused of something, replies that it wasn't him because he has "never been to Roswell."

Barry Goldwater, a U.S. senator from Arizona and also a 1964 Presidential candidate, was also interested in what the U.S. government knew about UFOs. In 1975, he apparently tried to get access to the building where UFO evidence was being held at Wright-Patterson Air Force Base and was denied. He later claimed in 1988 that he believed the government was hiding information about UFOs. He also said that he asked General Curtis Lemay if he could get inside the building at Wright-Patterson AFB, but Lemay denied his request and told him not to ask something like that again.

In 2004, Governor Bill Richardson of New Mexico claimed that the incident at Roswell was poorly explained and that he had tried to find out more about it but was told that it was classified.

During the impeachment investigation of Bill Clinton, led by Ken Starr, a copy of a book about the Roswell incident was taken from Clinton's personal library. Additionally, there exists a photo of Hillary Clinton walking while carrying a book. When the photo was enlarged and a barcode was scanned, it was determined that the book was entitled *Are We Alone?* UFO buffs and conspiracy theorists tried to show that the

Clintons were particularly interested in the possibility of a governmental cover-up of UFOs.

COVER-UPS AND PROJECT MOGUL

As pressure has been placed on United States governmental entities to reveal what happened at Roswell, the explanations have changed to meet the need. Originally, the crash debris recovery at the Brazel site was explained as being a weather balloon. Lots of weather balloons were released in the area at the time. Later, when it seemed that the material recovered could not have been a standard weather balloon because it was too large and the military would not have made a weather balloon incident classified, another story was presented that seemed to fit. Around 1994, the United States Air Force released declassified information stating that Project Mogul was in progress from 1947 to 1949. Project Mogul involved sending electronic detection devices up into the atmosphere via high-altitude balloons to monitor sounds which might indicate that the Soviet Union was conducting atomic bomb tests. It later was replaced by more accurate methods involving seismograph readings. Anyway, the Air Force claimed that a Project Mogul balloon was launched from Alamogordo, New Mexico on June 4, 1947 and that it later landed on the Foster Ranch to become misidentified as a flying saucer. Later, modifications had to be added to account for the reports of crashed craft and alien body recoveries. The Air Force said that there were occasions when routine military aircraft crashed and pilots had to be recovered. Also, there were incidents requiring the recovery of test pilots, and the experimental aircraft they were flying, and all information was classified. Then, there were the stories of recovered bodies that were non-human with various descriptions of the standard alien type. Once again, the Air Force came through by saying that during the period of the Roswell happenings, they tested a lot of parachutes and other devices involving the use of test dummies. The test dummies were normal human size and did not explain the four-foot-tall aliens with four fingers. Of course, that was remedied by the explanation that the bottom or fingers of the dummies were occasionally torn off, causing them to be shorter or missing fingers. The government cover-ups tended to adjust to the situation at hand, assuming there was a cover-up in the first place. One must remember that the government has never given us a reason to believe that they would do any such thing.

BOOKS, TELEVISION, AND POP CULTURE

The Roswell UFO incident is considered to be one of the top UFO investigations to ever happen. There have been many investigators that have worked on the story and a large number of books on the affair have been written. Some of the books that have been authored are as follows—

UFO Crash at Roswell by Kevin Randle and Donald Schmitt
The Truth About the UFO Crash at Roswell by Kevin Randle
    and Donald Schmitt
Crash at Corona: The U.S. Military Retrieval and Cover-up of a
    UFO by Stanton T. Friedman and Don Berliner
Top Secret/Majic: Operation Majestic-12 and the United States
    Government's UFO Cover-up by Stanton Friedman
Roswell: 52 Years of Unanswered Questions by Donald
    Schmitt and Thomas Carey
The Roswell UFO Crash: What They Don't Want You to Know
    by Kal K. Korff
The Real Roswell Crashed-Saucer Coverup by Philip J. Klass
The Day After Roswell by Philip J. Corso
The Roswell Legacy: The Untold Story of the First Military
    Officer at the 1947 Crash Site by Jesse Marcel, Jr. and
    Linda Marcel
Witness to Roswell: Unmasking the Government's Biggest
    Cover-up by Thomas Carey and Donald Schmitt
The Roswell Incident by Charles Berlitz and William Moore.

There are certainly many more.

There have also been a number of television documentaries on the subject—

The Roswell Incident (1995), directed by Tim Shawcross and
    starring many of the original witnesses
The Roswell Crash: Startling New Evidence (2002), directed by
    Melissa Jo Peltierire,
Six Days in Roswell (1998), directed by Timothy B. Johnson
Unsolved Mysteries—UFOs, hosted by Robert Stack
Do You Believe in Majic? (2004), directed by Paul Kimball
The History Channel—Where Are All the UFOs, directed by
    Scott Paddor
Stanton T. Friedman Is Real! (2002), directed by Paul
    Kimball.

A TV series entitled *Roswell*, produced and written by Jason Katims, is based on the incident. A number of comic books with the Roswell theme have also been written. Additionally, numerous magazines and newspapers articles have been published featuring articles about Roswell theories and recent developments.

A major spin-off of the Roswell incident is the *Roswell UFO Festival*. The festival first began on the 60th anniversary of the Roswell incident in 2007 and is held each year around the first of July. In 1992, Walter Haut and Glenn Dennis, key witnesses mentioned earlier in this book, got together and founded the International UFO Museum and Research Center at Roswell, NM.

Tourists, UFO enthusiasts, and researchers travel from all over the world to experience Roswell, see the museum, and to explore the area where it is believed that the crash happened.

INTL. UFO MUSEUM AND RESEARCH CENTER
ROSWELL, NEW MEXICO

When driving around Roswell, you are reminded of the Roswell UFO incident by what you observe—

A sign says *"UFO Parking,"*
A clock face reads *"We Are Not Alone,"*
An Arby's restaurant sign reads *"Aliens Welcome,"*
A McDonald's restaurant is shaped like a giant
flying saucer,

A diner has a metallic flying saucer embedded on
the outside front,
A business says *"Zone II Alien Headquarters,"*
A motel sign features a sleeping alien with the
words *"I feel at home,"*
The front of a Coke machine features an alien
drinking a bottle of coke,
A street light globe resembles the head of an alien,
complete with eyes, and
A Roswell phone directory features a picture of
an alien on the front.

CONCLUSION

If you are interested in exploring the mystery
of the Roswell UFO crash of 1947 or any other
weird occurrence of similar nature, I recommend
reading and researching through books,
magazines, newspapers, and the internet. The
internet is a good source, but you need to beware
of the misinformation that is sometimes found
there. Keep an open mind about what you learn.
If you have the opportunity, travel to Roswell
and visit the International UFO Museum and
Research Center and the Roswell UFO Festival.
Don't expect to talk to actual witnesses unless
you happen to find Walter Haut or Glenn Dennis
walking around the museum. Don't venture onto
private property without permission from

landowners. Digging and searching for evidence is something for the professionals. However, keeping your eyes on the sky is something you might consider because strange crafts have been known to make an appearance. Hopefully, after all these years something will turn up to prove that it wasn't all about some weather balloon, top secret Mogul surveillance balloons, or a bunch of crash dummies.

Before closing this book, I will add something. I attended Ordnance Elementary during the 1950s at Point Pleasant, West Virginia. The school was originally built to educate the children of scientists who worked on projects dealing with the World War II effort. Several of my classmates had fathers who were always working away or were with the military. Quite often, someone in class would pack up and move away unexpectedly to be wherever their father was stationed. I was in the first grade when the teacher announced that there would be a "show and tell" the next day. On that day, a boy brought a shiny piece of metal to school and passed it around. He said that his father brought it home and that it came from an alien spacecraft!

THE END

Office Memorandum UNITED STATES GOVERNMENT

TO : DIRECTOR, FBI

DATE: March 22, 1950

FROM : GUY HOTTEL, SAC, WASHINGTON

SUBJECT: FLYING SAUCERS
INFORMATION CONCERNING

b7C
b7D

The following information was furnished to SA _____ by _____

An investigator for the Air Forces stated that three so-called
flying saucers had been recovered in New Mexico. They were
described as being circular in shape with raised centers, approxi-
mately 50 feet in diameter. Each one was occupied by three bodies
of human shape but only 3 feet tall, dressed in metallic cloth of
a very fine texture. Each body was bandaged in a manner similar
to the blackout suits used by speed flyers and test pilots.

b7C   According to Mr. _____ informant, the saucers were found in New
Mexico due to the fact that the Government has a very high-powered
radar set-up in that area and it is believed the radar interferes
with the controling mechanism of the saucers.

No further evaluation was attempted by SA _____ concerning the
above.

RHK:VIM

RECORDED - 3
INDEXED - 8

162-83894-209
MAR 28 1950
34

5 1 MAR 29 1950

FBI SPECIAL AGENT GUY HOTTEL MEMO
MENTIONS RECOVERY OF THREE FLYING SAUCERS

42

RAAF Captures Flying Saucer on Ranch in Roswell Region

No Details of Flying Disk Are Revealed

The intelligence office of the 509th Bombardment group at Roswell Army Air Field announced at noon today, that the field has come into possession of a flying saucer.

According to information released by the department, over authority of Maj. J. A. Marcel, intelligence officer, the disk was recovered on a ranch in the Roswell vicinity, after an unidentified rancher had notified Sheriff Geo. Wilcox, here, that he had found the instrument on his premises.

Major Marcel and a detail from his department went to the ranch and recovered the disk, it was stated.

After the intelligence officer here had inspected the instrument it was flown to higher headquarters. The intelligence office stated that no details of the saucer's construction or its appearance had been revealed.

Roswell Hardware Man and Wife Report Disk Seen

Mr. and Mrs. Dan Wilmot apparently were the only persons in Roswell who seen what they thought was a flying disk.

They were sitting on their porch at 105 South Penn. last Wednesday night at about ten o'clock when a large glowing object zoomed out of the sky from the southeast, going in a northwesterly direction at a high rate of speed. Wilmot called Mrs. Wilmot's attention to it and both ran down into the yard to watch. It was in sight less then a minute, perhaps 40 or 50 seconds, Wilmot estimated.

Wilmot said that it appeared to him to be about 1,500 feet high and going fast. He estimated between 400 and 500 miles per hour.

In appearance it looked oval in shape like two inverted saucers, faced mouth to mouth, or like two old type washbowls placed, together in the same fashion. The entire body glowed as though light were showing through from inside, though not like it would inside, though not like it would be if a light were merely underneath.

From where he stood Wilmot said that the object looked to be about 5 feet in size, and making allowance for the distance it was from town he figured that it must have been 15 to 20 feet in diameter, though this was just a guess.

Wilmot said that he heard no sound but that Mrs. Wilmot said she heard a swishing sound for a very short time.

The object came into view from the southeast and disappeared over the treetops in the general vicinity of six mile hill.

Wilmot, who is one of the most respected and reliable citizens in town, kept the story to himself hoping that someone else would come out and tell about having seen one, but finally today decided that he would go ahead and tell about it. The announcement that the RAAF was in possession of one came only a few minutes after he decided to release the details of what he had seen.

TEXT FROM NEWSPAPER FRONT PAGE
ROSWELL DAILY RECORD - JULY 8, 1947

OTHER BOOKS BY THE AUTHOR

Strange Encounters: UFOs, Aliens and Mothman
The Tale of the Mason County Mothman
If I Taught It
The Flatwoods Monster
What Happened at Roswell?
They Haunt the Winfield Cemetery
The Kecksburg UFO Incident
The Kelly-Hopkinsville UFO and Alien Shootout
The Rendlesham Forest UFO
The Cape Girardeau 1941 UFO Incident
The Aurora 1897 UFO-Alien Encounter
The Socorro UFO Close Encounter
Bigfoot: The West Virginia Foothold
The Shag Harbour UFO Puzzle
The Berwyn Mountain UFO
The Thomas Mantell UFO Encounter
Sis Linn: The Ghost of Glenville State College
The Arnoldsburg Molasses Monster (not in print)
The Spencer Black Walnut Monster (not in print)
Inside Haunted Spencer State Hospital
Bigfoot 2: The West Virginia Stomping Grounds
The Aztec Flying Saucer Affair
The Laredo UFO Crash
Bigfoot 3: The West Virginia Toehold
The Silver Bridge Tragedy
The Falcon Lake UFO Encounter
Sheepsquatch
Bigfoot 4: The West Virginia Footprint
Kentucky's Lake Herrington Monster

The Maury Island UFO Encounter
Return to Haunted Spencer State Hospital
Dogman: Michigan-Wisconsin-West Virginia
The Cash Landrum UFO Encounter
The Levelland UFO Case
Goatman
Ohio's Frogmen and Melon Heads
Beyond Haunted Spencer State Hospital
Bigfoot 5: The West Virginia Yeti
Devil Monkey
Crybaby Bridge
Spring-heeled Jack
Cemetery Ghost Hunting: An Investigative Approach
The Oceana Monster
Cemetery Ghost Hunting 2: More Investigations
History of Spencer State Hospital
The Jersey Devil
Haunted White House
Graveyard Ghost Hunting: The Search Continues
Bigfoot West Virginia
Haunted Highways USA
Abraham Lincoln: The Ghost Years
The Grafton Monster
Haunted Savannah
UFO Traffic Stop
The Snarly Yow
Mothman Territory: History and High Strangeness
Skunk Ape: Florida's Bigfoot
Krazy House: America's Haunted Asylums
Dover Demon and Pukwudgies
Rougarou: Louisiana's Werewolf